CW00408832

100
Story
Ideas
For Your
Novel

By Roxanne Crouse
darkwhimsicalart.com
darkwhimsicalart@gmail.com

One Hundred Story Ideas For Your Novel

Sometimes the well of ideas runs dry and an author needs help filling it again. This book was created to help fill that well and get you passed writer's block. You can use the listings as is, or you can use them as a starting point. You can combine two or more ideas together if you like.

Don't worry about copyright. All the ideas are free to use anyway you like. Maybe some of them will inspire a main character or the plot in your next novel. Use a 100 sided die or two ten sided dies to pick one at random.

Get more books like this at darkwhimsicalart.com

Copyright: 2021 by Roxanne Crouse

TAKE CARE AND ENJOY THE JOURNEY

QUICK LIST

One Hundred Story Ideas For Your Novel
   Take Care and enjoy the journey

Idea One: Create a new government agency and give it an acronym. Now write a story about the new agency.

Idea Two: Write a story about a character that sees secret messages everywhere. Is it true oR are they crazy?

Idea Three: Make up an interesting title, then write a story to go along with the title

Idea Four: Write about a character eating an alien food. Describe what that experience is like in detail.

Idea Five: Find an old hotel online, learn about it, and write a story evolving the hotel.

Idea Six: Write a scene or story where smell plays a vital role in the plot

Idea Seven: Write a story about a character that is obsessed with women's hair

Idea Eight: Write a story about a character with a phobia of cats

Idea Nine: Take an old fairy tale and change what happens.

Idea Ten: A character gets a seed from an alien. Write about what happens when the seed is planted.

Idea Eleven: Write about a character that is a psychopathic liar and everyone loves them

Idea Twelve: Write about an alien species that to humans looks part animal.

Idea Thirteen: Write a story where people start turning into cocoons. What comes out?

Idea Fourteen: Write a story where witchcraft, fortune telling, and psychic powers are real.

Idea Fifteen: Close your eyes and pick a random word in the dictionary. Turn that word into a story.

Idea Sixteen: Write a scene evolving an unusual proposal. Think outside the box.

Idea Seventeen: Write a story about a character that has a list of names. What is that list for?

Idea Eighteen: Find a strange news paper story and turn it into a fiction story

Idea Nineteen: Pick a random town and set a story in the town

Idea Twenty: Write a story that takes place at a Sega Crane Game building in Tokyo, Japan

Idea Twenty One: Envision the future a hundred years from now. Turn it into a story

Idea Twenty Two: The moon has cracked. How has that affected the earth?

Idea Twenty Three: Write a story about a woman in white ghost

Idea Twenty Four: Write a story that takes place at a haunted beach

Idea Twenty Five: Create a spell and then write a story involving the spell

Idea Twenty Six: Write about the spanish flu pandemic a hundred years ago

Idea Twenty Seven: Write a twist where two identical men in a town are unaware of each other

Idea Twenty Eight: Use the first interesting phrase you hear as a title and write a story

Idea Twenty nine: Put two characters who hate each other together and write a scene

Idea Thirty: Write about a character wearing a 1920s flapper dress

Idea Thirty one: Write about a character who thinks he has superpowers

Idea Thirty Two: Your main character gets sucked into a strange cult

Idea Thirty Three: Write about an anime fan who decides to move to Tokyo.

Idea Thirty Four: Write about thunder and lightning from the perspective of a cat

Idea Thirty Five: Take an old story and rewrite it into horror

Idea Thirty Six: What if fairies were real. What would everyday life be like?

Idea Thirty Seven: Take two of the prompts in this book and combine them together and start writing.

Idea Thirty Eight: Write about a character suffering from imposter syndrome.

Idea Thirty Nine: Create a prophecy and then write a story around that prophecy

Idea Forty: Write a scene about a character enjoying a dessert in a sexual way

Idea Forty One: Write about a normal day on a spaceship. Get real detailed.

Idea Forty Two: Write about owning a car that is painted in the blackest black paint.

Idea Forty Three: Make up a holiday. Now write a scene happening during that holiday.

Idea Forty Four: Write a scene where what the character is saying does not match what they are thinking in their head

Idea Forty Five: Give two characters opposite problems and write a scene where they debate it out

Idea Forty Six: Write about a person who can bring people back from the dead

Idea Forty Seven: Write a scene that involves the color you dislike the most

Idea Forty Eight: Write about a character whose entire online life if faked

Idea Forty Nine: Write about a character who wakes up every night at 3:33am.

Idea Fifty: Write from a point of view you have never written from before.

Idea Fifty One: Write a story with the title, "Maybe This Time."

Idea Fifty Two: Write a story with a twist and then deliver a second twist

Idea Fifty Three: Write a scene where the Social Security Office lost the character's birth certificate and refuse to do anything about it

Idea Fifty Four: One character rear ends another character's car. Write what happens between the two characters. Make it interesting.

Idea Fifty Five: Write about a character who works in a hotel that is under construction. The character suffers from migraines.

Idea Fifty Six: Write about a character who dislikes her life, but is doing nothing to change it.

Idea Fifty Seven: A character steps into a fairy ring after being warned not to. What happens?

Idea Fifty Eight: Write about a world that has become over populated by robot vending machines.

Idea Fifty Nine: Write about something you heard other people talking about.

Idea Sixty: Write about a character trying to figure out what another character is thinking about.

Idea Sixty One: Write about a world where all the animals died off.

Idea Sixty Two: Write about a character that thinks they are about to get their wish, but doesn't.

Idea Sixty Three: What interesting dreams have you had lately? Write a story about it.

Idea Sixty Four: Write a story where a character finds out he has a secret twin.

Idea Sixty Five: Whatever embarrasses your character the most, write a scene where it happens.

Idea Sixty Six: Write a story where memory is the most important aspect of the society.

Idea Sixty Seven: Hell Is Other People. Right a scene where other people make it hell for your character

Idea Sixty Eight: Write a story about an alien living as a human

Idea Sixty Nine: Create an interesting magic system and then write a story about it.

PRompt Seventy: Try to invent something that changes your fictional world

Idea Seventy one: Some Christians visit the house of a buddhist. What happens?

Idea Seventy Two: Scientists discover new planets everyday. Write about one of them.

Idea Seventy Three: Write about a world where they can renovate people's minds.

Idea Seventy Four: Someone in your character's family has disappeared. Write about what happened.

Idea Seventy Five: Write about a world where people are forced to be happy

Idea Seventy Six: Write about a character who is obsessed with being an entrepreneur at any cost.

Idea Seventy Seven: Turn a very happy fairy tale into a nightmare.

Idea Seventy Eight: Write a character who is thankful for something they shouldn't be thankful about.

Idea Seventy Nine: If you have never written comedy then write a comedy. If you have never written a horror write horror.

Idea Eighty: There is a box on the porch that is moving. What does your character do?

PRompt Eighty one: Your character is a demon in a house trying to possess someone.

Idea Eighty Two: What fate could be worse than death? Write that story.

Idea Eighty Three: Write an emotional scene that will make a reader cry.

Idea Eighty Four: Write a story about the mythological creature the phoenix.

Idea Eighty Five: Find an interesting sign and make a story out of it.

Idea Eighty Six: Write about a terrible sound that your character can't stand.

Idea Eighty Seven: Your character is part of an elite club. What happens when this club meets?

Idea Eighty Eight: Your character is lost in a foregn country. How does she cope?

Idea Eighty Nine: A law is passed where everyone has to have the same hair color. Your character doesn't want that hair color.

Idea Ninety: Your character sent their child to summer camp. Each letter from the child gets stranger and stranger.

Idea Ninety One: Create a new horror monster and write a story about it.

Idea Ninety Two: Your character is at a masquerade party and keeps seeing a very strange masked person.

Idea Ninety Three: Pick an obstacle you want to overcome in life. Now write a character that does overcome that obstacle.

Idea Ninety Four: Your character decides to go toa party they were not invited to. What happens?

Idea Ninety Five: Write about something traumatic that happened to you.

Idea Ninety Six: Write about food in some way and how it affects the characters.

Idea Ninety Seven: Pick eight random words and use all of them in your story.

Idea Ninety Eight: Write a character that has gotten devastating news.

Idea Ninety Nine: Write about a Neighbor that keeps spying on your character.

Idea One Hundred: Your character's day has been very strange. Write what happens on that day.

Thank You so much for Purchasing my Book. I hope you found the Ideas lurking Inside useful.

Idea One: Create a new government agency and give it an acronym. Now write a story about the new agency.

Story Outline

Act 1

MEET THE PROTAGONIST

MAIN THEME GETS MENTIONED

INCITING INCIDENT 10% IN

DEBATE TO DO THE THING OR NOT

Act 2

SECONDARY STORY INTRODUCED

FINDING THE WAY

MIDPOINT

ANTAGONIST WINS

ALL SEEMS LOST

DARKEST HOUR

Act 3

A-HA MOMENT

FINALE

NEW LIFE OF THE PROTAGONIST

Idea Two: Write a story about a character that sees secret messages everywhere. Is it true or are they crazy?

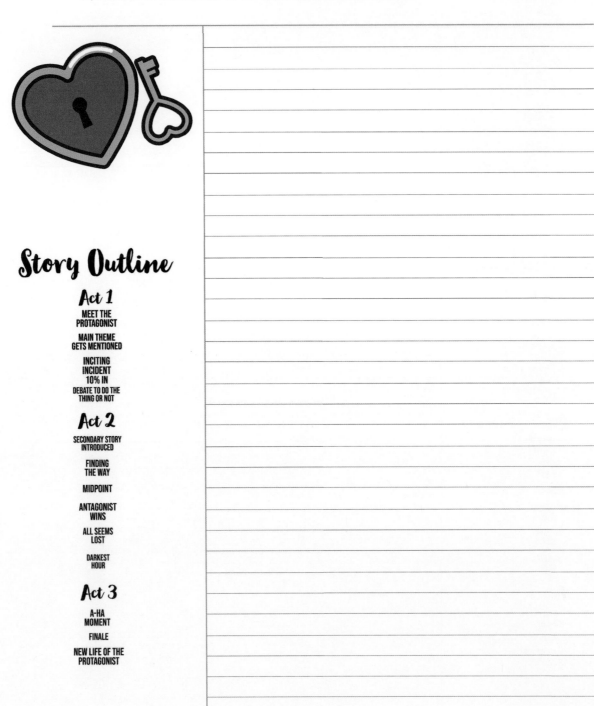

Story Outline

Act 1

MEET THE
PROTAGONIST

MAIN THEME
GETS MENTIONED

INCITING
INCIDENT
10% IN

DEBATE TO DO THE
THING OR NOT

Act 2

SECONDARY STORY
INTRODUCED

FINDING
THE WAY

MIDPOINT

ANTAGONIST
WINS

ALL SEEMS
LOST

DARKEST
HOUR

Act 3

A-HA
MOMENT

FINALE

NEW LIFE OF THE
PROTAGONIST

Idea Three: Make up an interesting title, then write a story to go along with the title

Story Outline

Act 1

MEET THE PROTAGONIST

MAIN THEME GETS MENTIONED

INCITING INCIDENT 10% IN

DEBATE TO DO THE THING OR NOT

Act 2

SECONDARY STORY INTRODUCED

FINDING THE WAY

MIDPOINT

ANTAGONIST WINS

ALL SEEMS LOST

DARKEST HOUR

Act 3

A-HA MOMENT

FINALE

NEW LIFE OF THE PROTAGONIST

Idea Four: Write about a character eating an alien food.

Describe what that experience is like in detail.

Story Outline

Act 1

MEET THE PROTAGONIST

MAIN THEME GETS MENTIONED

INCITING INCIDENT 10% IN

DEBATE TO DO THE THING OR NOT

Act 2

SECONDARY STORY INTRODUCED

FINDING THE WAY

MIDPOINT

ANTAGONIST WINS

ALL SEEMS LOST

DARKEST HOUR

Act 3

A-HA MOMENT

FINALE

NEW LIFE OF THE PROTAGONIST

Idea Five: Find an old hotel online, learn about it, and write a story evolving the hotel.

Story Outline

Act 1

MEET THE
PROTAGONIST

MAIN THEME
GETS MENTIONED

INCITING
INCIDENT
10% IN

DEBATE TO DO THE
THING OR NOT

Act 2

SECONDARY STORY
INTRODUCED

FINDING
THE WAY

MIDPOINT

ANTAGONIST
WINS

ALL SEEMS
LOST

DARKEST
HOUR

Act 3

A-HA
MOMENT

FINALE

NEW LIFE OF THE
PROTAGONIST

Idea Six: Write a scene or story where smell plays a vital role in the plot

Story Outline

Act 1

MEET THE
PROTAGONIST

MAIN THEME
GETS MENTIONED

INCITING
INCIDENT
10% IN

DEBATE TO DO THE
THING OR NOT

Act 2

SECONDARY STORY
INTRODUCED

FINDING
THE WAY

MIDPOINT

ANTAGONIST
WINS

ALL SEEMS
LOST

DARKEST
HOUR

Act 3

A-HA
MOMENT

FINALE

NEW LIFE OF THE
PROTAGONIST

Idea Seven: Write a story about a character that is obsessed with women's hair

Story Outline

Act 1

MEET THE PROTAGONIST

MAIN THEME GETS MENTIONED

INCITING INCIDENT 10% IN

DEBATE TO DO THE THING OR NOT

Act 2

SECONDARY STORY INTRODUCED

FINDING THE WAY

MIDPOINT

ANTAGONIST WINS

ALL SEEMS LOST

DARKEST HOUR

Act 3

A-HA MOMENT

FINALE

NEW LIFE OF THE PROTAGONIST

Idea Eight: Write a story about a character with a phobia of cats

Story Outline

Act 1

MEET THE PROTAGONIST

MAIN THEME GETS MENTIONED

INCITING INCIDENT 10% IN

DEBATE TO DO THE THING OR NOT

Act 2

SECONDARY STORY INTRODUCED

FINDING THE WAY

MIDPOINT

ANTAGONIST WINS

ALL SEEMS LOST

DARKEST HOUR

Act 3

A-HA MOMENT

FINALE

NEW LIFE OF THE PROTAGONIST

Idea Nine: Take an old fairy tale and change what happens.

Story Outline

Act 1

MEET THE PROTAGONIST

MAIN THEME GETS MENTIONED

INCITING INCIDENT 10% IN

DEBATE TO DO THE THING OR NOT

Act 2

SECONDARY STORY INTRODUCED

FINDING THE WAY

MIDPOINT

ANTAGONIST WINS

ALL SEEMS LOST

DARKEST HOUR

Act 3

A-HA MOMENT

FINALE

NEW LIFE OF THE PROTAGONIST

Idea Ten: A character gets a seed from an alien.

Write about what happens when the seed is planted.

Story Outline

Act 1

MEET THE
PROTAGONIST

MAIN THEME
GETS MENTIONED

INCITING
INCIDENT
10% IN

DEBATE TO DO THE
THING OR NOT

Act 2

SECONDARY STORY
INTRODUCED

FINDING
THE WAY

MIDPOINT

ANTAGONIST
WINS

ALL SEEMS
LOST

DARKEST
HOUR

Act 3

A-HA
MOMENT

FINALE

NEW LIFE OF THE
PROTAGONIST

Idea Eleven: Write about a character that is a psychopathic liar and everyone loves them

Story Outline

Act 1

MEET THE PROTAGONIST

MAIN THEME GETS MENTIONED

INCITING INCIDENT 10% IN

DEBATE TO DO THE THING OR NOT

Act 2

SECONDARY STORY INTRODUCED

FINDING THE WAY

MIDPOINT

ANTAGONIST WINS

ALL SEEMS LOST

DARKEST HOUR

Act 3

A-HA MOMENT

FINALE

NEW LIFE OF THE PROTAGONIST

Idea Twelve: Write about an alien species that to humans looks part animal.

Story Outline

Act 1

MEET THE PROTAGONIST

MAIN THEME GETS MENTIONED

INCITING INCIDENT 10% IN

DEBATE TO DO THE THING OR NOT

Act 2

SECONDARY STORY INTRODUCED

FINDING THE WAY

MIDPOINT

ANTAGONIST WINS

ALL SEEMS LOST

DARKEST HOUR

Act 3

A-HA MOMENT

FINALE

NEW LIFE OF THE PROTAGONIST

Idea Thirteen: Write a story where people start turning into cocoons. What comes out?

Story Outline

Act 1

MEET THE PROTAGONIST

MAIN THEME GETS MENTIONED

INCITING INCIDENT 10% IN

DEBATE TO DO THE THING OR NOT

Act 2

SECONDARY STORY INTRODUCED

FINDING THE WAY

MIDPOINT

ANTAGONIST WINS

ALL SEEMS LOST

DARKEST HOUR

Act 3

A-HA MOMENT

FINALE

NEW LIFE OF THE PROTAGONIST

Idea Fourteen: Write a story where witchcraft, fortune telling, and psychic powers are real.

Story Outline

Act 1

MEET THE
PROTAGONIST

MAIN THEME
GETS MENTIONED

INCITING
INCIDENT
10% IN

DEBATE TO DO THE
THING OR NOT

Act 2

SECONDARY STORY
INTRODUCED

FINDING
THE WAY

MIDPOINT

ANTAGONIST
WINS

ALL SEEMS
LOST

DARKEST
HOUR

Act 3

A-HA
MOMENT

FINALE

NEW LIFE OF THE
PROTAGONIST

Idea Fifteen: Close your eyes and pick a random word in the dictionary. Turn that word into a story.

Story Outline

Act 1
MEET THE PROTAGONIST

MAIN THEME GETS MENTIONED

INCITING INCIDENT 10% IN

DEBATE TO DO THE THING OR NOT

Act 2
SECONDARY STORY INTRODUCED

FINDING THE WAY

MIDPOINT

ANTAGONIST WINS

ALL SEEMS LOST

DARKEST HOUR

Act 3
A-HA MOMENT

FINALE

NEW LIFE OF THE PROTAGONIST

Idea Sixteen: Write a scene evolving an unusual proposal. Think outside the box.

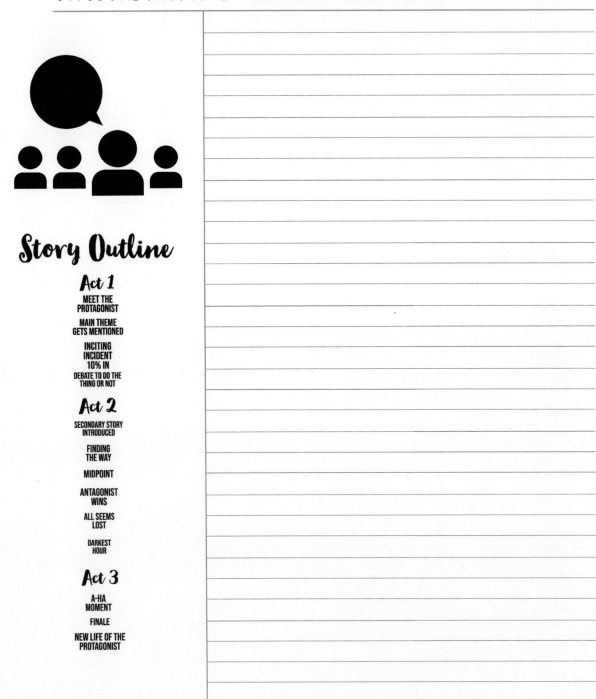

Story Outline

Act 1

MEET THE PROTAGONIST

MAIN THEME GETS MENTIONED

INCITING INCIDENT 10% IN

DEBATE TO DO THE THING OR NOT

Act 2

SECONDARY STORY INTRODUCED

FINDING THE WAY

MIDPOINT

ANTAGONIST WINS

ALL SEEMS LOST

DARKEST HOUR

Act 3

A-HA MOMENT

FINALE

NEW LIFE OF THE PROTAGONIST

Idea Seventeen: Write a story about a character that has a list of names. What is that list for?

Story Outline

Act 1
MEET THE
PROTAGONIST

MAIN THEME
GETS MENTIONED

INCITING
INCIDENT
10% IN

DEBATE TO DO THE
THING OR NOT

Act 2
SECONDARY STORY
INTRODUCED

FINDING
THE WAY

MIDPOINT

ANTAGONIST
WINS

ALL SEEMS
LOST

DARKEST
HOUR

Act 3
A-HA
MOMENT

FINALE

NEW LIFE OF THE
PROTAGONIST

Idea Eighteen: Find a strange news paper story and turn it into a fiction story

Story Outline

Act 1

MEET THE PROTAGONIST

MAIN THEME GETS MENTIONED

INCITING INCIDENT 10% IN

DEBATE TO DO THE THING OR NOT

Act 2

SECONDARY STORY INTRODUCED

FINDING THE WAY

MIDPOINT

ANTAGONIST WINS

ALL SEEMS LOST

DARKEST HOUR

Act 3

A-HA MOMENT

FINALE

NEW LIFE OF THE PROTAGONIST

Idea Nineteen: Pick a random town and set a story in the town

Story Outline

Act 1

MEET THE
PROTAGONIST

MAIN THEME
GETS MENTIONED

INCITING
INCIDENT
10% IN

DEBATE TO DO THE
THING OR NOT

Act 2

SECONDARY STORY
INTRODUCED

FINDING
THE WAY

MIDPOINT

ANTAGONIST
WINS

ALL SEEMS
LOST

DARKEST
HOUR

Act 3

A-HA
MOMENT

FINALE

NEW LIFE OF THE
PROTAGONIST

Idea Twenty: Write a story that takes place at a Sega Crane Game building in Tokyo, Japan

Story Outline

Act 1

MEET THE PROTAGONIST

MAIN THEME GETS MENTIONED

INCITING INCIDENT 10% IN

DEBATE TO DO THE THING OR NOT

Act 2

SECONDARY STORY INTRODUCED

FINDING THE WAY

MIDPOINT

ANTAGONIST WINS

ALL SEEMS LOST

DARKEST HOUR

Act 3

A-HA MOMENT

FINALE

NEW LIFE OF THE PROTAGONIST

Idea Twenty One: Envision the future a hundred years from now.
Turn it into a story

Story Outline

Act 1

MEET THE PROTAGONIST

MAIN THEME GETS MENTIONED

INCITING INCIDENT 10% IN

DEBATE TO DO THE THING OR NOT

Act 2

SECONDARY STORY INTRODUCED

FINDING THE WAY

MIDPOINT

ANTAGONIST WINS

ALL SEEMS LOST

DARKEST HOUR

Act 3

A-HA MOMENT

FINALE

NEW LIFE OF THE PROTAGONIST

Idea Twenty Two: The moon has cracked. How has that affected the earth?

Story Outline

Act 1
MEET THE PROTAGONIST

MAIN THEME GETS MENTIONED

INCITING INCIDENT 10% IN

DEBATE TO DO THE THING OR NOT

Act 2
SECONDARY STORY INTRODUCED

FINDING THE WAY

MIDPOINT

ANTAGONIST WINS

ALL SEEMS LOST

DARKEST HOUR

Act 3
A-HA MOMENT

FINALE

NEW LIFE OF THE PROTAGONIST

Idea Twenty Three: Write a story about a woman in white ghost

Story Outline

Act 1

MEET THE PROTAGONIST

MAIN THEME GETS MENTIONED

INCITING INCIDENT 10% IN

DEBATE TO DO THE THING OR NOT

Act 2

SECONDARY STORY INTRODUCED

FINDING THE WAY

MIDPOINT

ANTAGONIST WINS

ALL SEEMS LOST

DARKEST HOUR

Act 3

A-HA MOMENT

FINALE

NEW LIFE OF THE PROTAGONIST

Story Outline

Act 1

MEET THE PROTAGONIST

MAIN THEME GETS MENTIONED

INCITING INCIDENT 10% IN

DEBATE TO DO THE THING OR NOT

Act 2

SECONDARY STORY INTRODUCED

FINDING THE WAY

MIDPOINT

ANTAGONIST WINS

ALL SEEMS LOST

DARKEST HOUR

Act 3

A-HA MOMENT

FINALE

NEW LIFE OF THE PROTAGONIST

Idea Twenty Five: Create a spell and then write a story involving the spell

Story Outline

Act 1

MEET THE PROTAGONIST

MAIN THEME GETS MENTIONED

INCITING INCIDENT 10% IN

DEBATE TO DO THE THING OR NOT

Act 2

SECONDARY STORY INTRODUCED

FINDING THE WAY

MIDPOINT

ANTAGONIST WINS

ALL SEEMS LOST

DARKEST HOUR

Act 3

A-HA MOMENT

FINALE

NEW LIFE OF THE PROTAGONIST

Idea Twenty Six: Write about the spanish flu pandemic a hundred years ago

Story Outline

Act 1

MEET THE
PROTAGONIST

MAIN THEME
GETS MENTIONED

INCITING
INCIDENT
10% IN

DEBATE TO DO THE
THING OR NOT

Act 2

SECONDARY STORY
INTRODUCED

FINDING
THE WAY

MIDPOINT

ANTAGONIST
WINS

ALL SEEMS
LOST

DARKEST
HOUR

Act 3

A-HA
MOMENT

FINALE

NEW LIFE OF THE
PROTAGONIST

Idea Twenty Seven: Write a twist where two identical men in a town are unaware of each other

Story Outline

Act 1
MEET THE PROTAGONIST

MAIN THEME GETS MENTIONED

INCITING INCIDENT 10% IN

DEBATE TO DO THE THING OR NOT

Act 2
SECONDARY STORY INTRODUCED

FINDING THE WAY

MIDPOINT

ANTAGONIST WINS

ALL SEEMS LOST

DARKEST HOUR

Act 3
A-HA MOMENT

FINALE

NEW LIFE OF THE PROTAGONIST

Idea Twenty Eight: Use the first interesting phrase you hear as a title and write a story

Story Outline

Act 1

MEET THE PROTAGONIST

MAIN THEME GETS MENTIONED

INCITING INCIDENT 10% IN

DEBATE TO DO THE THING OR NOT

Act 2

SECONDARY STORY INTRODUCED

FINDING THE WAY

MIDPOINT

ANTAGONIST WINS

ALL SEEMS LOST

DARKEST HOUR

Act 3

A-HA MOMENT

FINALE

NEW LIFE OF THE PROTAGONIST

Idea Twenty nine: Put two characters who hate each other together and write a scene

Story Outline

Act 1

MEET THE PROTAGONIST

MAIN THEME GETS MENTIONED

INCITING INCIDENT 10% IN

DEBATE TO DO THE THING OR NOT

Act 2

SECONDARY STORY INTRODUCED

FINDING THE WAY

MIDPOINT

ANTAGONIST WINS

ALL SEEMS LOST

DARKEST HOUR

Act 3

A-HA MOMENT

FINALE

NEW LIFE OF THE PROTAGONIST

Idea Thirty: Write about a character wearing a 1920s flapper dress

Story Outline

Act 1
MEET THE PROTAGONIST

MAIN THEME GETS MENTIONED

INCITING INCIDENT 10% IN

DEBATE TO DO THE THING OR NOT

Act 2
SECONDARY STORY INTRODUCED

FINDING THE WAY

MIDPOINT

ANTAGONIST WINS

ALL SEEMS LOST

DARKEST HOUR

Act 3
A-HA MOMENT

FINALE

NEW LIFE OF THE PROTAGONIST

Idea Thirty one: Write about a character who thinks he has superpowers

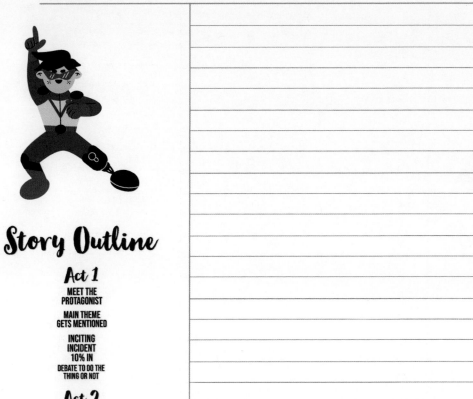

Story Outline

Act 1

MEET THE
PROTAGONIST

MAIN THEME
GETS MENTIONED

INCITING
INCIDENT
10% IN

DEBATE TO DO THE
THING OR NOT

Act 2

SECONDARY STORY
INTRODUCED

FINDING
THE WAY

MIDPOINT

ANTAGONIST
WINS

ALL SEEMS
LOST

DARKEST
HOUR

Act 3

A-HA
MOMENT

FINALE

NEW LIFE OF THE
PROTAGONIST

Idea Thirty Two: Your main character gets sucked into a strange cult

Story Outline

Act 1

MEET THE PROTAGONIST

MAIN THEME GETS MENTIONED

INCITING INCIDENT 10% IN

DEBATE TO DO THE THING OR NOT

Act 2

SECONDARY STORY INTRODUCED

FINDING THE WAY

MIDPOINT

ANTAGONIST WINS

ALL SEEMS LOST

DARKEST HOUR

Act 3

A-HA MOMENT

FINALE

NEW LIFE OF THE PROTAGONIST

Idea Thirty Three: Write about an anime fan who decides to move to Tokyo.

Story Outline

Act 1
MEET THE PROTAGONIST

MAIN THEME GETS MENTIONED

INCITING INCIDENT 10% IN

DEBATE TO DO THE THING OR NOT

Act 2
SECONDARY STORY INTRODUCED

FINDING THE WAY

MIDPOINT

ANTAGONIST WINS

ALL SEEMS LOST

DARKEST HOUR

Act 3
A-HA MOMENT

FINALE

NEW LIFE OF THE PROTAGONIST

Idea Thirty Four: Write about thunder and lightning from the perspective of a cat

Story Outline

Act 1

MEET THE PROTAGONIST

MAIN THEME GETS MENTIONED

INCITING INCIDENT 10% IN

DEBATE TO DO THE THING OR NOT

Act 2

SECONDARY STORY INTRODUCED

FINDING THE WAY

MIDPOINT

ANTAGONIST WINS

ALL SEEMS LOST

DARKEST HOUR

Act 3

A-HA MOMENT

FINALE

NEW LIFE OF THE PROTAGONIST

Idea Thirty Five: Take an old story and rewrite it into horror

Story Outline

Act 1

MEET THE
PROTAGONIST

MAIN THEME
GETS MENTIONED

INCITING
INCIDENT
10% IN

DEBATE TO DO THE
THING OR NOT

Act 2

SECONDARY STORY
INTRODUCED

FINDING
THE WAY

MIDPOINT

ANTAGONIST
WINS

ALL SEEMS
LOST

DARKEST
HOUR

Act 3

A-HA
MOMENT

FINALE

NEW LIFE OF THE
PROTAGONIST

Idea Thirty Six: What if fairies were real. What would everyday life be like?

Story Outline

Act 1

MEET THE PROTAGONIST

MAIN THEME GETS MENTIONED

INCITING INCIDENT 10% IN

DEBATE TO DO THE THING OR NOT

Act 2

SECONDARY STORY INTRODUCED

FINDING THE WAY

MIDPOINT

ANTAGONIST WINS

ALL SEEMS LOST

DARKEST HOUR

Act 3

A-HA MOMENT

FINALE

NEW LIFE OF THE PROTAGONIST

Idea Thirty Seven: Take two of the prompts in this book and combine them together and start writing.

Story Outline

Act 1

MEET THE
PROTAGONIST

MAIN THEME
GETS MENTIONED

INCITING
INCIDENT
10% IN

DEBATE TO DO THE
THING OR NOT

Act 2

SECONDARY STORY
INTRODUCED

FINDING
THE WAY

MIDPOINT

ANTAGONIST
WINS

ALL SEEMS
LOST

DARKEST
HOUR

Act 3

A-HA
MOMENT

FINALE

NEW LIFE OF THE
PROTAGONIST

Idea Thirty Eight: Write about a character suffering from imposter syndrome.

Story Outline

Act 1

MEET THE PROTAGONIST

MAIN THEME GETS MENTIONED

INCITING INCIDENT 10% IN

DEBATE TO DO THE THING OR NOT

Act 2

SECONDARY STORY INTRODUCED

FINDING THE WAY

MIDPOINT

ANTAGONIST WINS

ALL SEEMS LOST

DARKEST HOUR

Act 3

A-HA MOMENT

FINALE

NEW LIFE OF THE PROTAGONIST

Idea Thirty Nine: Create a prophecy and then write a story around that prophecy

Story Outline

Act 1

MEET THE PROTAGONIST

MAIN THEME GETS MENTIONED

INCITING INCIDENT 10% IN

DEBATE TO DO THE THING OR NOT

Act 2

SECONDARY STORY INTRODUCED

FINDING THE WAY

MIDPOINT

ANTAGONIST WINS

ALL SEEMS LOST

DARKEST HOUR

Act 3

A-HA MOMENT

FINALE

NEW LIFE OF THE PROTAGONIST

Idea Forty: Write a scene about a character enjoying a dessert in a sexual way

Story Outline

Act 1

MEET THE
PROTAGONIST

MAIN THEME
GETS MENTIONED

INCITING
INCIDENT
10% IN

DEBATE TO DO THE
THING OR NOT

Act 2

SECONDARY STORY
INTRODUCED

FINDING
THE WAY

MIDPOINT

ANTAGONIST
WINS

ALL SEEMS
LOST

DARKEST
HOUR

Act 3

A-HA
MOMENT

FINALE

NEW LIFE OF THE
PROTAGONIST

Idea Forty One: Write about a normal day on a spaceship. Get real detailed.

Story Outline

Act 1

MEET THE PROTAGONIST

MAIN THEME GETS MENTIONED

INCITING INCIDENT 10% IN

DEBATE TO DO THE THING OR NOT

Act 2

SECONDARY STORY INTRODUCED

FINDING THE WAY

MIDPOINT

ANTAGONIST WINS

ALL SEEMS LOST

DARKEST HOUR

Act 3

A-HA MOMENT

FINALE

NEW LIFE OF THE PROTAGONIST

Idea Forty Two: Write about owning a car that is painted in the blackest black paint.

Story Outline

Act 1

MEET THE
PROTAGONIST

MAIN THEME
GETS MENTIONED

INCITING
INCIDENT
10% IN

DEBATE TO DO THE
THING OR NOT

Act 2

SECONDARY STORY
INTRODUCED

FINDING
THE WAY

MIDPOINT

ANTAGONIST
WINS

ALL SEEMS
LOST

DARKEST
HOUR

Act 3

A-HA
MOMENT

FINALE

NEW LIFE OF THE
PROTAGONIST

Idea Forty Three: Make up a holiday. Now write a scene happening during that holiday.

Story Outline

Act 1

MEET THE
PROTAGONIST

MAIN THEME
GETS MENTIONED

INCITING
INCIDENT
10% IN

DEBATE TO DO THE
THING OR NOT

Act 2

SECONDARY STORY
INTRODUCED

FINDING
THE WAY

MIDPOINT

ANTAGONIST
WINS

ALL SEEMS
LOST

DARKEST
HOUR

Act 3

A-HA
MOMENT

FINALE

NEW LIFE OF THE
PROTAGONIST

Idea Forty Four: Write a scene where what the character is saying does not match what they are thinking in their head

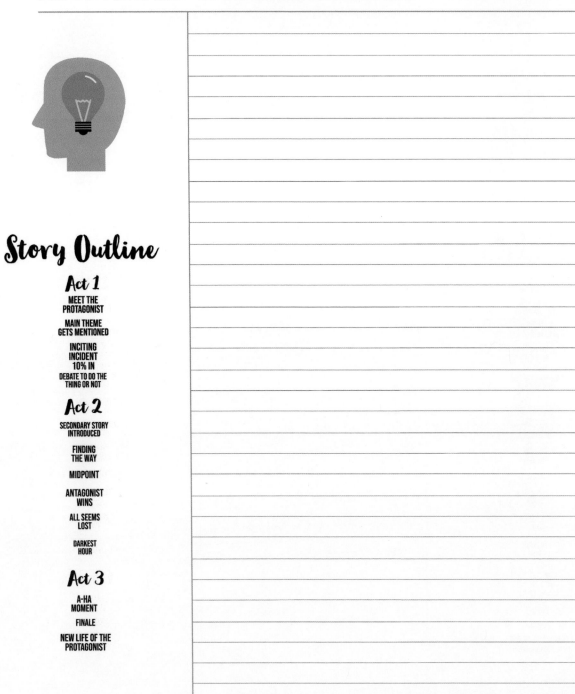

Story Outline

Act 1

MEET THE PROTAGONIST

MAIN THEME GETS MENTIONED

INCITING INCIDENT 10% IN

DEBATE TO DO THE THING OR NOT

Act 2

SECONDARY STORY INTRODUCED

FINDING THE WAY

MIDPOINT

ANTAGONIST WINS

ALL SEEMS LOST

DARKEST HOUR

Act 3

A-HA MOMENT

FINALE

NEW LIFE OF THE PROTAGONIST

Idea Forty Five: Give two characters opposite problems

and write a scene where they debate it out

Story Outline

Act 1

MEET THE PROTAGONIST

MAIN THEME GETS MENTIONED

INCITING INCIDENT 10% IN

DEBATE TO DO THE THING OR NOT

Act 2

SECONDARY STORY INTRODUCED

FINDING THE WAY

MIDPOINT

ANTAGONIST WINS

ALL SEEMS LOST

DARKEST HOUR

Act 3

A-HA MOMENT

FINALE

NEW LIFE OF THE PROTAGONIST

Idea Forty Six: Write about a person who can bring people back from the dead

Story Outline

Act 1

MEET THE PROTAGONIST

MAIN THEME GETS MENTIONED

INCITING INCIDENT 10% IN

DEBATE TO DO THE THING OR NOT

Act 2

SECONDARY STORY INTRODUCED

FINDING THE WAY

MIDPOINT

ANTAGONIST WINS

ALL SEEMS LOST

DARKEST HOUR

Act 3

A-HA MOMENT

FINALE

NEW LIFE OF THE PROTAGONIST

Idea Forty Seven: Write a scene that involves the color you dislike the most

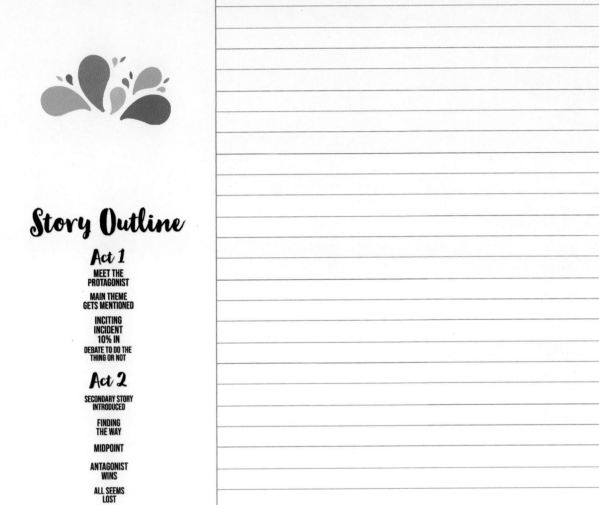

Story Outline

Act 1
MEET THE PROTAGONIST

MAIN THEME GETS MENTIONED

INCITING INCIDENT 10% IN

DEBATE TO DO THE THING OR NOT

Act 2
SECONDARY STORY INTRODUCED

FINDING THE WAY

MIDPOINT

ANTAGONIST WINS

ALL SEEMS LOST

DARKEST HOUR

Act 3
A-HA MOMENT

FINALE

NEW LIFE OF THE PROTAGONIST

Idea Forty Eight: Write about a character whose entire online life if faked

Story Outline

Act 1

MEET THE
PROTAGONIST

MAIN THEME
GETS MENTIONED

INCITING
INCIDENT
10% IN

DEBATE TO DO THE
THING OR NOT

Act 2

SECONDARY STORY
INTRODUCED

FINDING
THE WAY

MIDPOINT

ANTAGONIST
WINS

ALL SEEMS
LOST

DARKEST
HOUR

Act 3

A-HA
MOMENT

FINALE

NEW LIFE OF THE
PROTAGONIST

Idea Forty Nine: Write about a character who wakes up every night at 3:33am.

Story Outline

Act 1

MEET THE PROTAGONIST

MAIN THEME GETS MENTIONED

INCITING INCIDENT 10% IN

DEBATE TO DO THE THING OR NOT

Act 2

SECONDARY STORY INTRODUCED

FINDING THE WAY

MIDPOINT

ANTAGONIST WINS

ALL SEEMS LOST

DARKEST HOUR

Act 3

A-HA MOMENT

FINALE

NEW LIFE OF THE PROTAGONIST

Idea Fifty: Write from a point of view you have never written from before.

Story Outline

Act 1

MEET THE
PROTAGONIST

MAIN THEME
GETS MENTIONED

INCITING
INCIDENT
10% IN

DEBATE TO DO THE
THING OR NOT

Act 2

SECONDARY STORY
INTRODUCED

FINDING
THE WAY

MIDPOINT

ANTAGONIST
WINS

ALL SEEMS
LOST

DARKEST
HOUR

Act 3

A-HA
MOMENT

FINALE

NEW LIFE OF THE
PROTAGONIST

Idea Fifty One: Write a story with the title, "Maybe This Time."

Story Outline

Act 1

MEET THE PROTAGONIST

MAIN THEME GETS MENTIONED

INCITING INCIDENT 10% IN

DEBATE TO DO THE THING OR NOT

Act 2

SECONDARY STORY INTRODUCED

FINDING THE WAY

MIDPOINT

ANTAGONIST WINS

ALL SEEMS LOST

DARKEST HOUR

Act 3

A-HA MOMENT

FINALE

NEW LIFE OF THE PROTAGONIST

Idea Fifty Two: Write a story with a twist and then deliver a second twist

Story Outline

Act 1

MEET THE PROTAGONIST

MAIN THEME GETS MENTIONED

INCITING INCIDENT 10% IN

DEBATE TO DO THE THING OR NOT

Act 2

SECONDARY STORY INTRODUCED

FINDING THE WAY

MIDPOINT

ANTAGONIST WINS

ALL SEEMS LOST

DARKEST HOUR

Act 3

A-HA MOMENT

FINALE

NEW LIFE OF THE PROTAGONIST

Idea Fifty Three: Write a scene where the Social Security Office lost the character's birth certificate and refuse to do anything about it

Story Outline

Act 1

MEET THE
PROTAGONIST

MAIN THEME
GETS MENTIONED

INCITING
INCIDENT
10% IN
DEBATE TO DO THE
THING OR NOT

Act 2

SECONDARY STORY
INTRODUCED

FINDING
THE WAY

MIDPOINT

ANTAGONIST
WINS

ALL SEEMS
LOST

DARKEST
HOUR

Act 3

A-HA
MOMENT

FINALE

NEW LIFE OF THE
PROTAGONIST

Idea Fifty Four: One character rear ends another character's car. Write what happens between the two characters. Make it interesting.

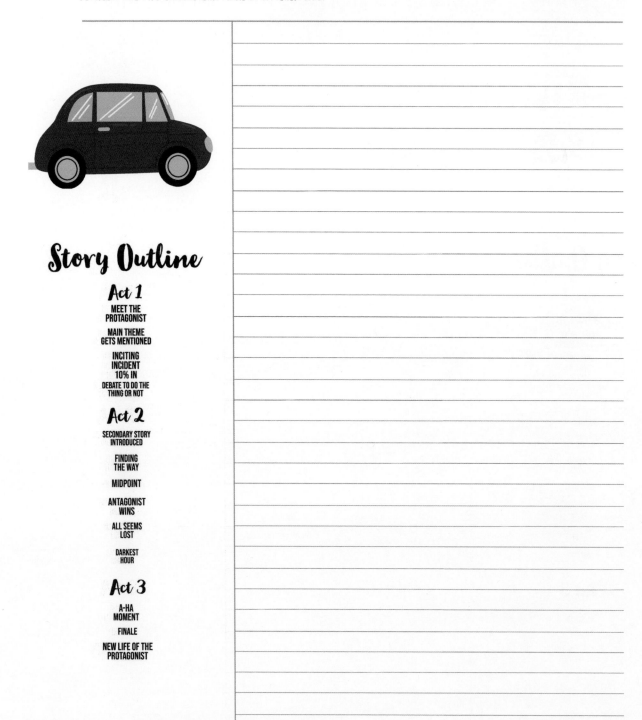

Story Outline

Act 1

MEET THE PROTAGONIST

MAIN THEME GETS MENTIONED

INCITING INCIDENT 10% IN

DEBATE TO DO THE THING OR NOT

Act 2

SECONDARY STORY INTRODUCED

FINDING THE WAY

MIDPOINT

ANTAGONIST WINS

ALL SEEMS LOST

DARKEST HOUR

Act 3

A-HA MOMENT

FINALE

NEW LIFE OF THE PROTAGONIST

Idea Fifty Five: Write about a character who works in a hotel that is
under construction. The character suffers from migraines.

Story Outline

Act 1

MEET THE
PROTAGONIST

MAIN THEME
GETS MENTIONED

INCITING
INCIDENT
10% IN

DEBATE TO DO THE
THING OR NOT

Act 2

SECONDARY STORY
INTRODUCED

FINDING
THE WAY

MIDPOINT

ANTAGONIST
WINS

ALL SEEMS
LOST

DARKEST
HOUR

Act 3

A-HA
MOMENT

FINALE

NEW LIFE OF THE
PROTAGONIST

Idea Fifty Six: Write about a character who dislikes her life, but is doing nothing to change it.

Story Outline

Act 1

MEET THE PROTAGONIST

MAIN THEME GETS MENTIONED

INCITING INCIDENT 10% IN

DEBATE TO DO THE THING OR NOT

Act 2

SECONDARY STORY INTRODUCED

FINDING THE WAY

MIDPOINT

ANTAGONIST WINS

ALL SEEMS LOST

DARKEST HOUR

Act 3

A-HA MOMENT

FINALE

NEW LIFE OF THE PROTAGONIST

Idea Fifty Seven: A character steps into a fairy ring after being warned not to. What happens?

Story Outline

Act 1

MEET THE PROTAGONIST

MAIN THEME GETS MENTIONED

INCITING INCIDENT 10% IN

DEBATE TO DO THE THING OR NOT

Act 2

SECONDARY STORY INTRODUCED

FINDING THE WAY

MIDPOINT

ANTAGONIST WINS

ALL SEEMS LOST

DARKEST HOUR

Act 3

A-HA MOMENT

FINALE

NEW LIFE OF THE PROTAGONIST

Idea Fifty Eight: Write about a world that has become over populated by robot vending machines.

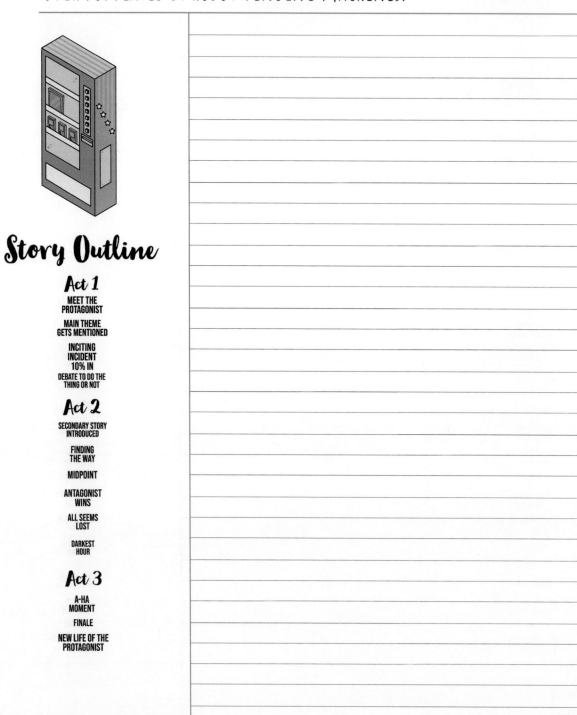

Story Outline

Act 1
MEET THE PROTAGONIST

MAIN THEME GETS MENTIONED

INCITING INCIDENT 10% IN

DEBATE TO DO THE THING OR NOT

Act 2
SECONDARY STORY INTRODUCED

FINDING THE WAY

MIDPOINT

ANTAGONIST WINS

ALL SEEMS LOST

DARKEST HOUR

Act 3
A-HA MOMENT

FINALE

NEW LIFE OF THE PROTAGONIST

Idea Fifty Nine: Write about something you heard other people talking about.

Story Outline

Act 1

MEET THE PROTAGONIST

MAIN THEME GETS MENTIONED

INCITING INCIDENT 10% IN

DEBATE TO DO THE THING OR NOT

Act 2

SECONDARY STORY INTRODUCED

FINDING THE WAY

MIDPOINT

ANTAGONIST WINS

ALL SEEMS LOST

DARKEST HOUR

Act 3

A-HA MOMENT

FINALE

NEW LIFE OF THE PROTAGONIST

Idea Sixty: Write about a character trying to figure out what another character is thinking about.

Story Outline

Act 1
MEET THE PROTAGONIST

MAIN THEME GETS MENTIONED

INCITING INCIDENT 10% IN

DEBATE TO DO THE THING OR NOT

Act 2
SECONDARY STORY INTRODUCED

FINDING THE WAY

MIDPOINT

ANTAGONIST WINS

ALL SEEMS LOST

DARKEST HOUR

Act 3
A-HA MOMENT

FINALE

NEW LIFE OF THE PROTAGONIST

Idea Sixty One: Write about a world where all the animals died off.

Story Outline

Act 1

MEET THE
PROTAGONIST

MAIN THEME
GETS MENTIONED

INCITING
INCIDENT
10% IN

DEBATE TO DO THE
THING OR NOT

Act 2

SECONDARY STORY
INTRODUCED

FINDING
THE WAY

MIDPOINT

ANTAGONIST
WINS

ALL SEEMS
LOST

DARKEST
HOUR

Act 3

A-HA
MOMENT

FINALE

NEW LIFE OF THE
PROTAGONIST

Idea Sixty Two: Write about a character that thinks they are about to get their wish, but doesn't.

Story Outline

Act 1

MEET THE
PROTAGONIST

MAIN THEME
GETS MENTIONED

INCITING
INCIDENT
10% IN

DEBATE TO DO THE
THING OR NOT

Act 2

SECONDARY STORY
INTRODUCED

FINDING
THE WAY

MIDPOINT

ANTAGONIST
WINS

ALL SEEMS
LOST

DARKEST
HOUR

Act 3

A-HA
MOMENT

FINALE

NEW LIFE OF THE
PROTAGONIST

Idea Sixty Three: What interesting dreams have you had lately? Write a story about it.

Story Outline

Act 1

MEET THE
PROTAGONIST

MAIN THEME
GETS MENTIONED

INCITING
INCIDENT
10% IN

DEBATE TO DO THE
THING OR NOT

Act 2

SECONDARY STORY
INTRODUCED

FINDING
THE WAY

MIDPOINT

ANTAGONIST
WINS

ALL SEEMS
LOST

DARKEST
HOUR

Act 3

A-HA
MOMENT

FINALE

NEW LIFE OF THE
PROTAGONIST

Idea Sixty Four: Write a story where a character finds out he has a secret twin.

Story Outline

Act 1

MEET THE PROTAGONIST

MAIN THEME GETS MENTIONED

INCITING INCIDENT 10% IN

DEBATE TO DO THE THING OR NOT

Act 2

SECONDARY STORY INTRODUCED

FINDING THE WAY

MIDPOINT

ANTAGONIST WINS

ALL SEEMS LOST

DARKEST HOUR

Act 3

A-HA MOMENT

FINALE

NEW LIFE OF THE PROTAGONIST

Idea Sixty Five: Whatever embarrasses your character the most, write a scene where it happens.

Story Outline

Act 1

MEET THE PROTAGONIST

MAIN THEME GETS MENTIONED

INCITING INCIDENT 10% IN

DEBATE TO DO THE THING OR NOT

Act 2

SECONDARY STORY INTRODUCED

FINDING THE WAY

MIDPOINT

ANTAGONIST WINS

ALL SEEMS LOST

DARKEST HOUR

Act 3

A-HA MOMENT

FINALE

NEW LIFE OF THE PROTAGONIST

Idea Sixty Six: Write a story where memory is the most important aspect of the society.

Story Outline

Act 1

MEET THE PROTAGONIST

MAIN THEME GETS MENTIONED

INCITING INCIDENT 10% IN

DEBATE TO DO THE THING OR NOT

Act 2

SECONDARY STORY INTRODUCED

FINDING THE WAY

MIDPOINT

ANTAGONIST WINS

ALL SEEMS LOST

DARKEST HOUR

Act 3

A-HA MOMENT

FINALE

NEW LIFE OF THE PROTAGONIST

Idea Sixty Seven: Hell Is Other People. Right a scene where other people make it hell for your character

Story Outline

Act 1
MEET THE
PROTAGONIST

MAIN THEME
GETS MENTIONED

INCITING
INCIDENT
10% IN
DEBATE TO DO THE
THING OR NOT

Act 2
SECONDARY STORY
INTRODUCED

FINDING
THE WAY

MIDPOINT

ANTAGONIST
WINS

ALL SEEMS
LOST

DARKEST
HOUR

Act 3
A-HA
MOMENT

FINALE

NEW LIFE OF THE
PROTAGONIST

Story Outline

Act 1

MEET THE PROTAGONIST

MAIN THEME GETS MENTIONED

INCITING INCIDENT 10% IN

DEBATE TO DO THE THING OR NOT

Act 2

SECONDARY STORY INTRODUCED

FINDING THE WAY

MIDPOINT

ANTAGONIST WINS

ALL SEEMS LOST

DARKEST HOUR

Act 3

A-HA MOMENT

FINALE

NEW LIFE OF THE PROTAGONIST

Idea Sixty Nine: Create an interesting magic system and then write a story about it.

Story Outline

Act 1
MEET THE PROTAGONIST

MAIN THEME GETS MENTIONED

INCITING INCIDENT 10% IN

DEBATE TO DO THE THING OR NOT

Act 2
SECONDARY STORY INTRODUCED

FINDING THE WAY

MIDPOINT

ANTAGONIST WINS

ALL SEEMS LOST

DARKEST HOUR

Act 3
A-HA MOMENT

FINALE

NEW LIFE OF THE PROTAGONIST

PRompt Seventy: Try to invent something that changes your fictional world

Story Outline

Act 1

MEET THE PROTAGONIST

MAIN THEME GETS MENTIONED

INCITING INCIDENT 10% IN

DEBATE TO DO THE THING OR NOT

Act 2

SECONDARY STORY INTRODUCED

FINDING THE WAY

MIDPOINT

ANTAGONIST WINS

ALL SEEMS LOST

DARKEST HOUR

Act 3

A-HA MOMENT

FINALE

NEW LIFE OF THE PROTAGONIST

Idea Seventy one: Some Christians visit the house of a buddhist. What happens?

Story Outline

Act 1
MEET THE PROTAGONIST

MAIN THEME GETS MENTIONED

INCITING INCIDENT 10% IN

DEBATE TO DO THE THING OR NOT

Act 2
SECONDARY STORY INTRODUCED

FINDING THE WAY

MIDPOINT

ANTAGONIST WINS

ALL SEEMS LOST

DARKEST HOUR

Act 3
A-HA MOMENT

FINALE

NEW LIFE OF THE PROTAGONIST

Idea Seventy Two: Scientists discover new planets everyday. Write about one of them.

Story Outline

Act 1

MEET THE PROTAGONIST

MAIN THEME GETS MENTIONED

INCITING INCIDENT 10% IN

DEBATE TO DO THE THING OR NOT

Act 2

SECONDARY STORY INTRODUCED

FINDING THE WAY

MIDPOINT

ANTAGONIST WINS

ALL SEEMS LOST

DARKEST HOUR

Act 3

A-HA MOMENT

FINALE

NEW LIFE OF THE PROTAGONIST

Idea Seventy Three: Write about a world where they can renovate people's minds.

Story Outline

Act 1

MEET THE PROTAGONIST

MAIN THEME GETS MENTIONED

INCITING INCIDENT 10% IN

DEBATE TO DO THE THING OR NOT

Act 2

SECONDARY STORY INTRODUCED

FINDING THE WAY

MIDPOINT

ANTAGONIST WINS

ALL SEEMS LOST

DARKEST HOUR

Act 3

A-HA MOMENT

FINALE

NEW LIFE OF THE PROTAGONIST

Idea Seventy Four: Someone in your character's family has disappeared. Write about what happened.

Story Outline

Act 1

MEET THE
PROTAGONIST

MAIN THEME
GETS MENTIONED

INCITING
INCIDENT
10% IN

DEBATE TO DO THE
THING OR NOT

Act 2

SECONDARY STORY
INTRODUCED

FINDING
THE WAY

MIDPOINT

ANTAGONIST
WINS

ALL SEEMS
LOST

DARKEST
HOUR

Act 3

A-HA
MOMENT

FINALE

NEW LIFE OF THE
PROTAGONIST

Idea Seventy Five: Write about a world where people are forced to be happy

Story Outline

Act 1
MEET THE PROTAGONIST

MAIN THEME GETS MENTIONED

INCITING INCIDENT 10% IN

DEBATE TO DO THE THING OR NOT

Act 2
SECONDARY STORY INTRODUCED

FINDING THE WAY

MIDPOINT

ANTAGONIST WINS

ALL SEEMS LOST

DARKEST HOUR

Act 3
A-HA MOMENT

FINALE

NEW LIFE OF THE PROTAGONIST

Idea Seventy Six: Write about a character who is obsessed with being an entrepreneur at any cost.

Story Outline

Act 1

MEET THE
PROTAGONIST

MAIN THEME
GETS MENTIONED

INCITING
INCIDENT
10% IN

DEBATE TO DO THE
THING OR NOT

Act 2

SECONDARY STORY
INTRODUCED

FINDING
THE WAY

MIDPOINT

ANTAGONIST
WINS

ALL SEEMS
LOST

DARKEST
HOUR

Act 3

A-HA
MOMENT

FINALE

NEW LIFE OF THE
PROTAGONIST

Idea Seventy Seven: Turn a very happy fairy tale into a nightmare.

Story Outline

Act 1

MEET THE
PROTAGONIST

MAIN THEME
GETS MENTIONED

INCITING
INCIDENT
10% IN

DEBATE TO DO THE
THING OR NOT

Act 2

SECONDARY STORY
INTRODUCED

FINDING
THE WAY

MIDPOINT

ANTAGONIST
WINS

ALL SEEMS
LOST

DARKEST
HOUR

Act 3

A-HA
MOMENT

FINALE

NEW LIFE OF THE
PROTAGONIST

Idea Seventy Eight: Write a character who is thankful for something they shouldn't be thankful about.

THANK YOU

Story Outline

Act 1

MEET THE
PROTAGONIST

MAIN THEME
GETS MENTIONED

INCITING
INCIDENT
10% IN

DEBATE TO DO THE
THING OR NOT

Act 2

SECONDARY STORY
INTRODUCED

FINDING
THE WAY

MIDPOINT

ANTAGONIST
WINS

ALL SEEMS
LOST

DARKEST
HOUR

Act 3

A-HA
MOMENT

FINALE

NEW LIFE OF THE
PROTAGONIST

IDEA SEVENTY NINE: IF YOU HAVE NEVER WRITTEN COMEDY THEN WRITE A
COMEDY. IF YOU HAVE NEVER WRITTEN A HORROR WRITE HORROR.

Story Outline

Act 1

MEET THE
PROTAGONIST

MAIN THEME
GETS MENTIONED

INCITING
INCIDENT
10% IN

DEBATE TO DO THE
THING OR NOT

Act 2

SECONDARY STORY
INTRODUCED

FINDING
THE WAY

MIDPOINT

ANTAGONIST
WINS

ALL SEEMS
LOST

DARKEST
HOUR

Act 3

A-HA
MOMENT

FINALE

NEW LIFE OF THE
PROTAGONIST

Idea Eighty: There is a box on the porch that is moving.
What does your character do?

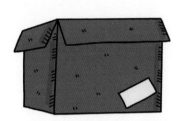

Story Outline

Act 1

MEET THE
PROTAGONIST

MAIN THEME
GETS MENTIONED

INCITING
INCIDENT
10% IN

DEBATE TO DO THE
THING OR NOT

Act 2

SECONDARY STORY
INTRODUCED

FINDING
THE WAY

MIDPOINT

ANTAGONIST
WINS

ALL SEEMS
LOST

DARKEST
HOUR

Act 3

A-HA
MOMENT

FINALE

NEW LIFE OF THE
PROTAGONIST

PRompt Eighty one: Your character is a demon in a house trying to possess someone.

Story Outline

Act 1
MEET THE PROTAGONIST

MAIN THEME GETS MENTIONED

INCITING INCIDENT 10% IN

DEBATE TO DO THE THING OR NOT

Act 2
SECONDARY STORY INTRODUCED

FINDING THE WAY

MIDPOINT

ANTAGONIST WINS

ALL SEEMS LOST

DARKEST HOUR

Act 3
A-HA MOMENT

FINALE

NEW LIFE OF THE PROTAGONIST

Idea Eighty Two: What fate could be worse than death? Write that story.

Story Outline

Act 1
MEET THE PROTAGONIST

MAIN THEME GETS MENTIONED

INCITING INCIDENT 10% IN

DEBATE TO DO THE THING OR NOT

Act 2
SECONDARY STORY INTRODUCED

FINDING THE WAY

MIDPOINT

ANTAGONIST WINS

ALL SEEMS LOST

DARKEST HOUR

Act 3
A-HA MOMENT

FINALE

NEW LIFE OF THE PROTAGONIST

Idea Eighty Three: Write an emotional scene that will make a reader cry.

Story Outline

Act 1

MEET THE PROTAGONIST

MAIN THEME GETS MENTIONED

INCITING INCIDENT 10% IN

DEBATE TO DO THE THING OR NOT

Act 2

SECONDARY STORY INTRODUCED

FINDING THE WAY

MIDPOINT

ANTAGONIST WINS

ALL SEEMS LOST

DARKEST HOUR

Act 3

A-HA MOMENT

FINALE

NEW LIFE OF THE PROTAGONIST

Idea Eighty Four: Write a story about the mythological creature the phoenix.

Story Outline

Act 1

MEET THE PROTAGONIST

MAIN THEME GETS MENTIONED

INCITING INCIDENT 10% IN

DEBATE TO DO THE THING OR NOT

Act 2

SECONDARY STORY INTRODUCED

FINDING THE WAY

MIDPOINT

ANTAGONIST WINS

ALL SEEMS LOST

DARKEST HOUR

Act 3

A-HA MOMENT

FINALE

NEW LIFE OF THE PROTAGONIST

Story Outline

Act 1

MEET THE PROTAGONIST

MAIN THEME GETS MENTIONED

INCITING INCIDENT 10% IN

DEBATE TO DO THE THING OR NOT

Act 2

SECONDARY STORY INTRODUCED

FINDING THE WAY

MIDPOINT

ANTAGONIST WINS

ALL SEEMS LOST

DARKEST HOUR

Act 3

A-HA MOMENT

FINALE

NEW LIFE OF THE PROTAGONIST

Story Outline

Act 1

MEET THE PROTAGONIST

MAIN THEME GETS MENTIONED

INCITING INCIDENT 10% IN

DEBATE TO DO THE THING OR NOT

Act 2

SECONDARY STORY INTRODUCED

FINDING THE WAY

MIDPOINT

ANTAGONIST WINS

ALL SEEMS LOST

DARKEST HOUR

Act 3

A-HA MOMENT

FINALE

NEW LIFE OF THE PROTAGONIST

Idea Eighty Seven: Your character is part of an elite club. What happens when this club meets?

Story Outline

Act 1

MEET THE PROTAGONIST

MAIN THEME GETS MENTIONED

INCITING INCIDENT 10% IN

DEBATE TO DO THE THING OR NOT

Act 2

SECONDARY STORY INTRODUCED

FINDING THE WAY

MIDPOINT

ANTAGONIST WINS

ALL SEEMS LOST

DARKEST HOUR

Act 3

A-HA MOMENT

FINALE

NEW LIFE OF THE PROTAGONIST

Idea Eighty Eight: Your character is lost in a foregn country. How does she cope?

Story Outline

Act 1

MEET THE
PROTAGONIST

MAIN THEME
GETS MENTIONED

INCITING
INCIDENT
10% IN

DEBATE TO DO THE
THING OR NOT

Act 2

SECONDARY STORY
INTRODUCED

FINDING
THE WAY

MIDPOINT

ANTAGONIST
WINS

ALL SEEMS
LOST

DARKEST
HOUR

Act 3

A-HA
MOMENT

FINALE

NEW LIFE OF THE
PROTAGONIST

IDEA EIGHTY NINE: A LAW IS PASSED WHERE EVERYONE HAS TO HAVE THE SAME HAIR COLOR. YOUR CHARACTER DOESN'T WANT THAT HAIR COLOR.

Story Outline

Act 1

MEET THE PROTAGONIST

MAIN THEME GETS MENTIONED

INCITING INCIDENT 10% IN

DEBATE TO DO THE THING OR NOT

Act 2

SECONDARY STORY INTRODUCED

FINDING THE WAY

MIDPOINT

ANTAGONIST WINS

ALL SEEMS LOST

DARKEST HOUR

Act 3

A-HA MOMENT

FINALE

NEW LIFE OF THE PROTAGONIST

Idea Ninety: Your character sent their child to summer camp.
Each letter from the child gets stranger and stranger.

Story Outline

Act 1

MEET THE PROTAGONIST

MAIN THEME GETS MENTIONED

INCITING INCIDENT 10% IN

DEBATE TO DO THE THING OR NOT

Act 2

SECONDARY STORY INTRODUCED

FINDING THE WAY

MIDPOINT

ANTAGONIST WINS

ALL SEEMS LOST

DARKEST HOUR

Act 3

A-HA MOMENT

FINALE

NEW LIFE OF THE PROTAGONIST

Idea Ninety One: Create a new horror monster and write a story about it.

Story Outline

Act 1
MEET THE
PROTAGONIST

MAIN THEME
GETS MENTIONED

INCITING
INCIDENT
10% IN

DEBATE TO DO THE
THING OR NOT

Act 2
SECONDARY STORY
INTRODUCED

FINDING
THE WAY

MIDPOINT

ANTAGONIST
WINS

ALL SEEMS
LOST

DARKEST
HOUR

Act 3
A-HA
MOMENT

FINALE

NEW LIFE OF THE
PROTAGONIST

Idea Ninety Two: Your character is at a masquerade party and keeps seeing a very strange masked person.

Story Outline

Act 1
MEET THE PROTAGONIST

MAIN THEME GETS MENTIONED

INCITING INCIDENT 10% IN

DEBATE TO DO THE THING OR NOT

Act 2
SECONDARY STORY INTRODUCED

FINDING THE WAY

MIDPOINT

ANTAGONIST WINS

ALL SEEMS LOST

DARKEST HOUR

Act 3
A-HA MOMENT

FINALE

NEW LIFE OF THE PROTAGONIST

Idea Ninety Three: Pick an obstacle you want to overcome in life.
Now write a character that does overcome that obstacle.

Story Outline

Act 1
MEET THE
PROTAGONIST

MAIN THEME
GETS MENTIONED

INCITING
INCIDENT
10% IN

DEBATE TO DO THE
THING OR NOT

Act 2
SECONDARY STORY
INTRODUCED

FINDING
THE WAY

MIDPOINT

ANTAGONIST
WINS

ALL SEEMS
LOST

DARKEST
HOUR

Act 3
A-HA
MOMENT

FINALE

NEW LIFE OF THE
PROTAGONIST

Idea Ninety Four: Your character decides to go to a party they were not invited to. What happens?

Story Outline

Act 1

MEET THE PROTAGONIST

MAIN THEME GETS MENTIONED

INCITING INCIDENT 10% IN

DEBATE TO DO THE THING OR NOT

Act 2

SECONDARY STORY INTRODUCED

FINDING THE WAY

MIDPOINT

ANTAGONIST WINS

ALL SEEMS LOST

DARKEST HOUR

Act 3

A-HA MOMENT

FINALE

NEW LIFE OF THE PROTAGONIST

Idea Ninety Five: Write about something traumatic that happened to you.

Story Outline

Act 1
MEET THE PROTAGONIST

MAIN THEME GETS MENTIONED

INCITING INCIDENT 10% IN

DEBATE TO DO THE THING OR NOT

Act 2
SECONDARY STORY INTRODUCED

FINDING THE WAY

MIDPOINT

ANTAGONIST WINS

ALL SEEMS LOST

DARKEST HOUR

Act 3
A-HA MOMENT

FINALE

NEW LIFE OF THE PROTAGONIST

Idea Ninety Six: Write about food in some way and how it affects the characters.

Story Outline

Act 1

MEET THE PROTAGONIST

MAIN THEME GETS MENTIONED

INCITING INCIDENT 10% IN

DEBATE TO DO THE THING OR NOT

Act 2

SECONDARY STORY INTRODUCED

FINDING THE WAY

MIDPOINT

ANTAGONIST WINS

ALL SEEMS LOST

DARKEST HOUR

Act 3

A-HA MOMENT

FINALE

NEW LIFE OF THE PROTAGONIST

Idea Ninety Seven: Pick eight random words and use all of them in your story.

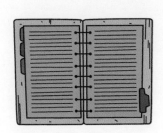

Story Outline

Act 1

MEET THE
PROTAGONIST

MAIN THEME
GETS MENTIONED

INCITING
INCIDENT
10% IN
DEBATE TO DO THE
THING OR NOT

Act 2

SECONDARY STORY
INTRODUCED

FINDING
THE WAY

MIDPOINT

ANTAGONIST
WINS

ALL SEEMS
LOST

DARKEST
HOUR

Act 3

A-HA
MOMENT

FINALE

NEW LIFE OF THE
PROTAGONIST

Idea Ninety Eight: Write a character that has gotten devastating news.

Story Outline

Act 1

MEET THE PROTAGONIST

MAIN THEME GETS MENTIONED

INCITING INCIDENT 10% IN

DEBATE TO DO THE THING OR NOT

Act 2

SECONDARY STORY INTRODUCED

FINDING THE WAY

MIDPOINT

ANTAGONIST WINS

ALL SEEMS LOST

DARKEST HOUR

Act 3

A-HA MOMENT

FINALE

NEW LIFE OF THE PROTAGONIST

Idea Ninety Nine: Write about a Neighbor that keeps spying on your character.

Story Outline

Act 1

MEET THE PROTAGONIST

MAIN THEME GETS MENTIONED

INCITING INCIDENT 10% IN

DEBATE TO DO THE THING OR NOT

Act 2

SECONDARY STORY INTRODUCED

FINDING THE WAY

MIDPOINT

ANTAGONIST WINS

ALL SEEMS LOST

DARKEST HOUR

Act 3

A-HA MOMENT

FINALE

NEW LIFE OF THE PROTAGONIST

Idea One Hundred: Your character's day has been very strange. Write what happens on that day.

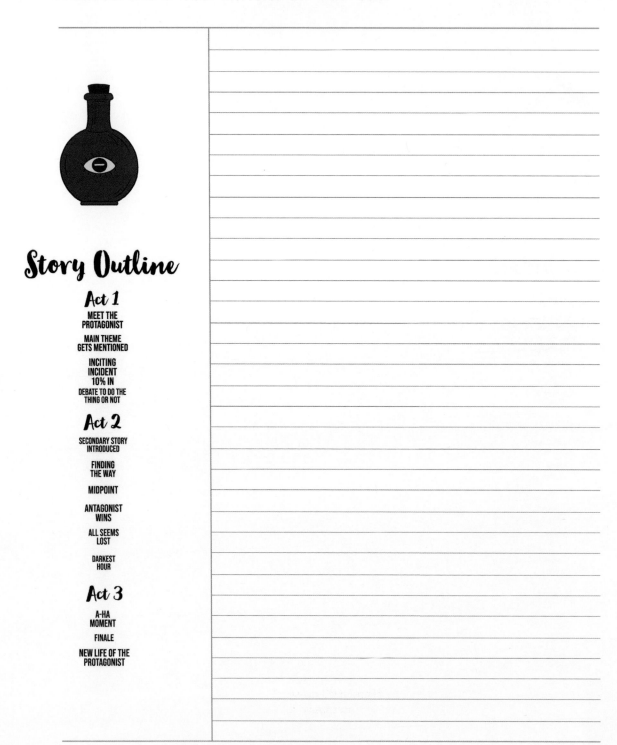

Story Outline

Act 1
MEET THE PROTAGONIST

MAIN THEME GETS MENTIONED

INCITING INCIDENT 10% IN

DEBATE TO DO THE THING OR NOT

Act 2
SECONDARY STORY INTRODUCED

FINDING THE WAY

MIDPOINT

ANTAGONIST WINS

ALL SEEMS LOST

DARKEST HOUR

Act 3
A-HA MOMENT

FINALE

NEW LIFE OF THE PROTAGONIST

Thank You so much for Purchasing my Book. I hope you found the Ideas lurking Inside useful.

darkwhimsicalart@gmail.com
Darkwhimsicalart.com

About The Author

Roxanne Crouse has been writing seriously since 2009 and has a few novels in the works and two published stories on Amazon. She lives with her husband and two cats that whisper all her best ideas into her ear. She also reviews and edits self-published books and helps promote self-published authors on her blog.

My Books on Amazon

Fortune
The Monster
Dark Whimsical Art Adult Coloring Book
Between The Lines
300 Creepy Dark Horror Writing Prompts
100 Horror Writing prompts
100 Creepy Writing Prompts
Dark Writing Prompts

100 First Lines For Your Novel
100 Writing Prompts For Your Novel
100 Story Ideas For Your Novel

Printed in Great Britain
by Amazon

10162585R10063